Introduction

Dear Parent,

At Teacher Created Materials, we believe every child is bright and brainy—and a little practice at home can go a long way! Although educational practices have changed over time, some key methods have stayed the same. Children need plenty of opportunities to practice skills and show what they know. The more they do, the more they can transfer their learning to everyday life—and future success!

Of course, there has to be a good purpose for the practice. That's where these activities come in. Created with the essential learning standards in mind, each activity page focuses on a particular concept, skill, or skill-set and provides students abundant opportunities to practice and achieve mastery.

You can feel confident using the activities prepared by teachers for learning at home, and your child will feel confident as they build skills and knowledge on their bright and brainy adventure.

Thank you for helping us to achieve our vision of creating a world in which children love to learn!

Your Friends at Teacher Created Materials

Common Core Standards Correlation Chart

Language Arts	
Reading: Foundational Skills	**Page(s)**
Count, pronounce, blend, and segment syllables in spoken words	4
Blend and segment onsets and rimes of single-syllable spoken words	5–7
Language Conventions	**Page(s)**
Print many upper- and lowercase letters	8–13
Use frequently occuring nouns and verbs	14–21
Form regular plural nouns	22–25
Understand and use question words	26–27
Use the most frequently occuring prepositions	28–29
Capitalize first word in sentence and the pronoun *I*	30–31
Recognize and name end punctuation	32–33
Write a letter or letters for most consonant and short-vowel sounds	34–39
Reading: Literature	**Page(s)**
Ask and answer questions about key details in text	40–42
Identify characters, settings, and major events in a story	43–44
Reading: Fluency	**Page(s)**
Read emergent-reader texts with purpose and understanding	45–46
Writing	**Page(s)**
Use a combination of drawing and writing to compose opinion pieces	47–48
Use a combination of drawing and writing to compose informative text	49–50
Use a combination of drawing and writing to narrate a single event	51–54
Speaking and Listening	**Page(s)**
Speak audibly and express thoughts, feelings, and ideas clearly	55–56

Mathematics	
Operations and Algebraic Thinking	**Page(s)**
Represent addition and subtraction with objects	57–60
Solve addition and subtraction word problems, and add and subtract within 10	61–69
Decompose numbers less than or equal to 10 into pairs	70–75
Number and Operations in Base Ten	**Page(s)**
Compose and decompose numbers from 11 to 19	75–76
Measurement and Data	**Page(s)**
Describe measurable attributes of objects	77, 79
Directly compare two objects with a measureable attribute	78, 80
Classify objects into given categories	81–84
Geometry	**Page(s)**
Describe objects in the environment using names of shapes	85–87
Correctly name shapes regardless of their orientations	88–91

Reading: Foundational Skills

Name: _____ Date: _____

How Many Parts?

Directions: Write 1 if the word has one part. Write 2 if the word has two parts.

❶	❷	❸
1		
❹	❺	❻

4

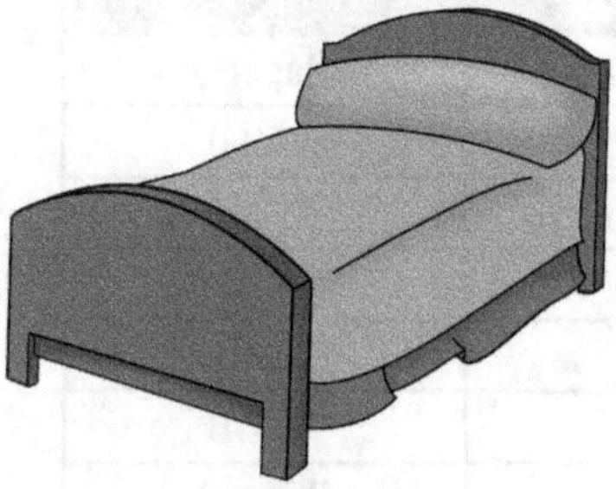

Reading: Foundational Skills

Name: _____ Date: _____

What Is That Sound?

Directions: Circle the pictures that start with the letter.

b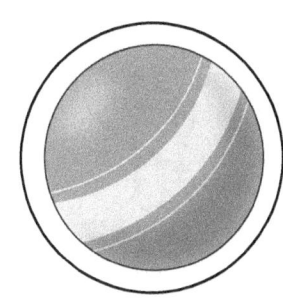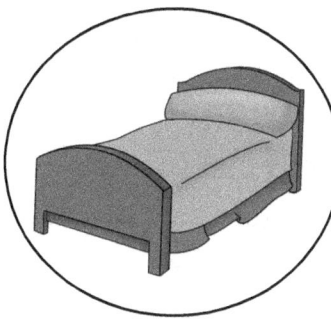

c

d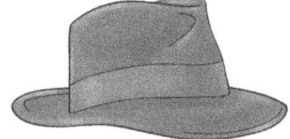

f

Reading: Foundational Skills

Name: _____ Date: _____

Name That Letter Sound

Directions: Circle the pictures that start with the letter.

Name: _____ Date: _____

Reading: Foundational Skills

Name More Letter Sounds

Directions: Circle the pictures that start with the letter.

s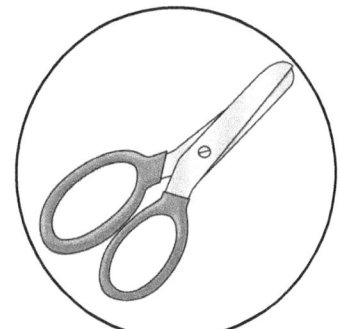

t

v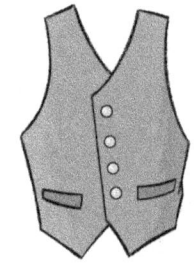

w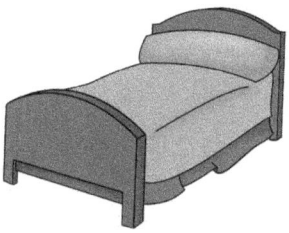

Language Conventions

Name: _____ Date: _____

Practice Your Letters

Directions: Trace the letters.

Language Conventions

Name: _____ Date: _____

Practice More Letters

Directions: Trace the letters.

9

Language Conventions

Name: _____ Date: _____

Practice Even More Letters

Directions: Trace the letters.

Language Conventions

Name: _____ Date: _____

Lots of Letters

Directions: Trace the letters.

Language Conventions

Name: _____ Date: _____

Trace More Letters

Directions: Trace the letters.

Language Conventions

Name: _____ Date: _____

Keep Tracing

Directions: Trace the letters.

Language Conventions

Name: _____ Date: _____

Which Word Is Right?

Directions: Choose the right word to finish the sentence.

1 That is a big ___bat___.
  hat   bat

2 The _____ is full.
  car   can

3 _____ has a bag.
  Dad   Mom

4 _____ is tall.
  Dad   Mom

Language Conventions

Name: _____ Date: _____

Choose the Right Word

Directions: Choose the right word to finish the sentence.

1. That is a big ___dog___.

hat   dog

2. The _____ has a toy.

baby   mom

3. The _____ is blue.

fish   bird

4. I ride the _____.

bus   car

15

Language Conventions

Name: _____ Date: _____

Which Word?

Directions: Choose the right word to finish the sentence.

1 The ___hen___ is white.
hen   dog

2 The pig is in the _____.
pen   car

3 The _____ is brown.
fish   house

4 The man has a _____.
dog   book

16

Language Conventions

Name: _____ Date: _____

Choose More Words

Directions: Choose the right word to finish the sentence.

❶ The ___ant___ is black.
ant green

❷ The eggs are on a _____ .
dish cup

❸ Birds live in a _____ .
net nest

❹ The dog is in a _____ .
tub bed

17

Language Conventions

Name: _____ Date: _____

Finish the Sentence

Directions: Choose the right word to finish the sentence.

① The duck ___flaps___.

flaps   begs

② The dog _____.

hops   wags

③ The fish _____.

digs   swims

④ The frog _____.

hops   hugs

Language Conventions

Name: _____ Date: _____

What Do These Pictures Say?

Directions: Choose the right word to finish the sentence.

1. The girl ___rides___ her bike.
rides runs

2. The boy _____ .
runs falls

3. The boy _____ .
digs naps

4. The girl _____ .
claps reads

19

Language Conventions

Name: _____ Date: _____

Read Carefully!

Directions: Choose the right word to finish the sentence.

①		The boat __moves__ . moves sinks
②		The girl _____ . skips stops
③		The bus _____ . claps stops
④		The plane _____ . falls flies

Language Conventions

Name: _____ Date: _____

Read These Carefully!

Directions: Choose the right word to finish the sentence.

1. The baby __plays__.

   naps plays

2. The mom _____.

   hugs sings

3. The boy _____.

   falls draws

4. The girl _____.

   rests grows

21

Language Conventions

Name: _____ Date: _____

One or Two?

The first picture says *hen*. The second picture says *hens* because there is more than one.

hen | hens

Directions: Circle the right word for each picture.

❶ pig   pigs

❷ hat   hats

❸ pan   pans

❹ sun   suns

Language Conventions

More Than One?

The first picture says *boy*. The second picture says *boys* because there is more than one.

Directions: Circle the right word for each picture.

Language Conventions

Name: _____ Date: _____

How Many in These?

The first picture says *box*. The second picture says *boxes* because there is more than one.

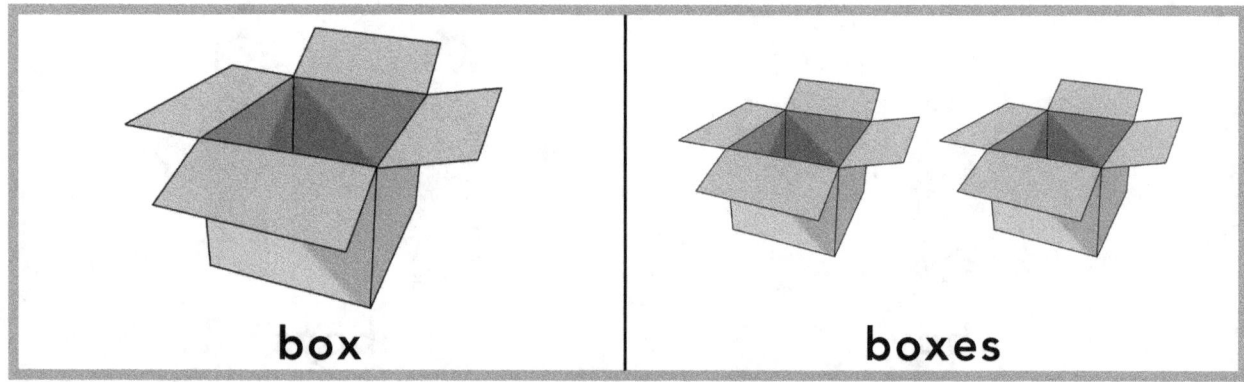

box   boxes

Directions: Circle the right word for each picture.

❶ fox   foxes

❷ watch   watches

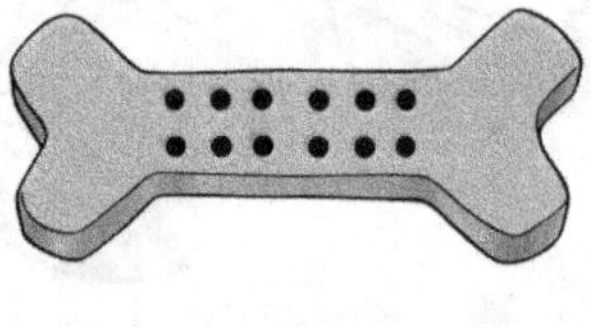

❸ bone   bones

❹ brush   brushes

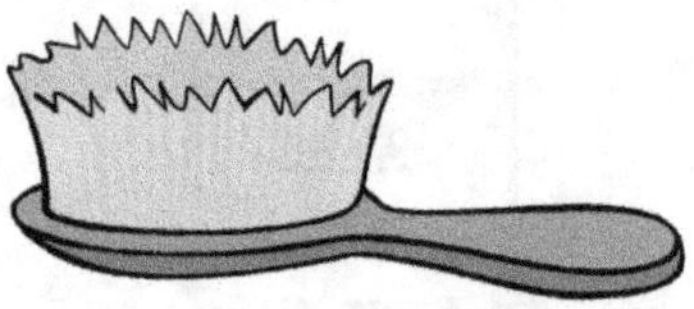

Language Conventions

Name: _____ Date: _____

More Plural Practice

The first picture says *ring*. The second picture says *rings* because there is more than one.

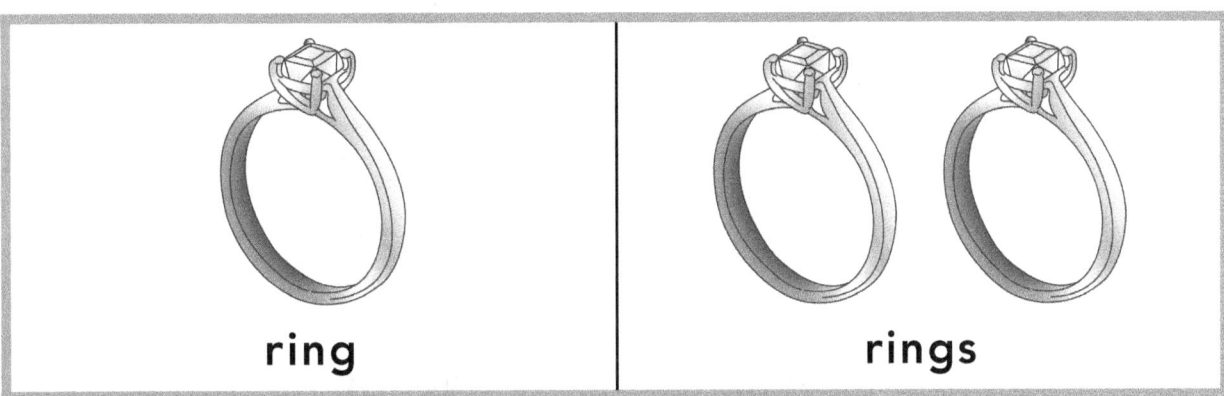

Directions: Circle the right word for each picture.

25

Language Conventions

Name: _____ Date: _____

Finish the Questions

Directions: Write the missing word for each question.

Who   What

1 _____What_____ is on the card?

2 _____ is the boy?

3 _____ does the boy have?

4 _____ has the cards?

Name: _____ Date: _____

Language Conventions

Finish More Questions

Directions: Write the missing word for each question.

Where   Who

1. _____Where_____ will they go?

2. _____ is stopped?

3. _____ is going?

4. _____ is the cone?

27

Language Conventions

Name: _____ Date: _____

Where Is It?

Directions: Write the missing word for each question.

on   by

① The food is _____ on _____ the tray.

② The peas are _____ the milk.

③ The cake is _____ the dish.

④ The meat is _____ the peas.

Language Conventions

Name: _____ Date: _____

Where Are They?

Directions: Write the missing word for each question.

in   by

① They are _____ in _____ the car.

② The girl is _____ the boy.

③ The boy is _____ the window.

④ They are _____ their seats.

Language Conventions

Name: _____ Date: _____

Capital Mistake

Directions: Put a check by the sentence with the capital letter mistake.

1 I have a dog. ☐

i have a dog. ✓

2 My dog has spots. ☐

my dog has spots. ☐

3 May i pet your dog? ☐

May I pet your dog? ☐

4 your dog is big! ☐

Your dog is big! ☐

Name: _____ Date: _____

Language Conventions

Capitalize It

Directions: Circle the words that need a capital letter.

(i) like my cats. they are fun. i give my cats toys. They like toys. max is white. he likes to play with yarn. Sox likes mice. she and Max are fun.

Language Conventions

Name: _____ Date: _____

Punctuate the Sentences

Sentences end with a period, question mark, or exclamation point. This is what each looks like:

.   ?   !

period   question mark   exclamation point

Directions: Circle the punctuation mark at the end of each sentence.

❶ Do you like apples?

.   (?)   !

❷ I love apples!

.   ?   !

❸ I have ten apples.

.   ?   !

❹ Can you count to ten?

.   ?   !

Language Conventions

Name: _____ Date: _____

Punctuate More Sentences

A sentence ends with a period, question mark, or exclamation point. This is what each looks like:

. ? !

period   question mark   exclamation point

Directions: Write a period, question mark, or exclamation point at the end of each sentence.

Do you know how to snap ____

I do ____

It can be hard ____

I like to snap ____

Language Conventions

Name: _____ Date: _____

Name the Short Vowels

Directions: Write the missing letter in the blank.

1

c __a__ n

2

m ___ p

3

b ___ g

4

b ___ g

Language Conventions

Name: _____ Date: _____

Name More Short Vowels

Directions: Write the missing letter in the blank.

1

b __a__ ll

2

l ___ d

3

d ___ ck

4

b ___ x

35

Language Conventions

Name: _____ Date: _____

Spelling Fun

Directions: Write the missing letter in the blank.

1. c _a_ r

2. s __ n

3. l __ g

4. c __ p

Language Conventions

Name: _____ Date: _____

More Spelling Words

Directions: Spell each picture.

1

___ ___ ___

e g g (traceable)

2

___ ___ ___

3

___ ___ ___

4

___ ___ ___

37

Language Conventions

Name: _____ Date: _____

Keep Spelling!

Directions: Spell each picture.

1

c a p

2

3

4

38

Language Conventions

Name: _____ Date: _____

Keep Spelling More Words!

Directions: Spell each picture.

1

f o o t

2

3

4

39

Find the Answers

Directions: Read the story. Then, answer the questions.

Pat likes to go to the park. He runs on the grass. He digs in the sand. He runs after a duck. He jumps up on a bench. Pat has fun!

1 Where does Pat go?
   a. for a walk
   b. to the sandbox
   c. to the park

2 What does Pat do on the grass?
   a. dig
   b. jump
   c. run

3 What does Pat run after?
   a. a duck
   b. a friend
   c. a cat

4 What does Pat jump up on?
   a. a bench
   b. the grass
   c. the sand

Reading: Literature

Name: _____ Date: _____

Questions to Answer

Directions: Read the story. Then, answer the questions.

Jan likes to help Mom. She puts soap in the tub. She adds toys. She adds water. Jan gets in. Mom says, "Jan! This does not help! Get the mop!"

❶ What does Jan like to do?
   a. take a bath
   b. help Mom
   c. mop up

❷ What did Jan put in the tub first?
   a. toys
   b. water
   c. soap

❸ What happens when Jan gets in the tub?
   a. Mom gets soap.
   b. The water spills.
   c. Mom mops.

❹ How do you think Mom feels?
   a. happy
   b. mad
   c. funny

Reading: Literature

Name: _____ Date: _____

Read the Answer

Directions: Read the story. Then, answer the questions.

Tim has a new pet. He did not get it at a pet shop. The pet came to Tim's house. The pet made a brown home near Tim's window. The pet is blue. Guess what it is!

❶ Tim did not get his pet at a pet shop. Why not?
  a. His mom gave it to him.
  b. It came to Tim's house.
  c. It came in the window.

❷ Where did it make its home?
  a. in Tim's room
  b. in Tim's box
  c. near Tim's window

❸ What color is the pet?
  a. gray
  b. blue
  c. brown

❹ The pet's home is in a tree. What kind of home is it?
  a. a nest
  b. a den
  c. a hole

42

Reading: Literature

Name: _____ Date: _____

Book Log

Directions: Read a book. Then, fill out the form below.

Title of book: _____

People in the book: _____

Places in the book: _____

Reading: Literature

Name: _____ Date: _____

Opposite Characters

Directions: Read a fairy tale. Choose two characters. Use words from the list to show how they are different.

> big or little   fast or slow   sad or happy
> boy or girl   good or bad

Character One	Character Two
_____	_____

Reading: Fluency

Name: _____ Date: _____

Be a Great Reader!

Directions: Try these ideas to be a good reader.

- Do not skip words you do not know. Ask for help and get them right next time.

- Read in the characters' voices.

- Read in a loud or soft voice.

- Read like you are on the radio.

- Read and record the book. Play it for someone in your family.

- Read the book like a chant.

- Read in a silly voice.

- Read like it is a great movie.

Reading: Fluency

Name: _____ Date: _____

More Tips for Being a Great Reader

Directions: Find a partner. Try these ideas to be a good reader.

- Read one page aloud. Have your partner read the next page.

- Read in the characters' voices.

- Read the book aloud together.

- One reads the book. The other acts it out.

- Turn the book into a play. Add music.

- Have a good reader read part of the book. Then, read it the same way.

- Take turns making up new endings.

- Be television reporters and read the book aloud.

Name: _____ Date: _____

My Good Book!

Directions: Write about why you like a book.

Title of book: _____

This is why I like the book: _____

_____
_____
_____
_____
_____
_____
_____
_____
_____
_____

Name: _____ Date: _____

My Book Review

Directions: Write about why you did not like a book.

Title of book: _____

This is why I did not like the book: _____

_____

_____

_____

_____

_____

_____

_____

_____

_____

_____

_____

Name: _____ Date: _____

About a Pet

Directions: Write sentences to tell about a pet.

Kind of Pet

_____

_____

_____

_____

Name of Pet

_____

_____

_____

_____

What It Eats

_____

_____

_____

_____

Best Thing About It

_____

_____

_____

_____

Writing

Name: _____ Date: _____

My Review

Directions: Write sentences to tell about a book or movie.

Name of Book or Movie

Setting

Main Character

Why I Like It

Name: _____ Date: _____

My Best Day

Directions: Write about your best day. The questions will help you.

❶ How did you feel when you woke up?

_____
_____
_____

❷ What did you do after you got out of bed?

_____
_____
_____

❸ What was the first thing that made your day great?

_____
_____
_____

❹ What was the last thing that made your day great?

_____
_____
_____

Writing

Name: _____ Date: _____

My Funny Day

Directions: Write about a funny day. The questions will help you.

1 Where were you?

_____
_____
_____
_____

2 Who was with you?

_____
_____
_____
_____

3 What was the first thing that made your day funny?

_____
_____
_____
_____

4 What was the second thing that made your day funny?

_____
_____
_____
_____

Name: _____ Date: _____

Writing Ideas

Directions: On a separate sheet of paper, try some of these ideas to help you be a better writer.

- Write an ad for a toy.

- Write a book of wishes.

- Write a cartoon book.

- Write a comic strip book.

- Write a favorite foods list.

- Write a grocery list for a cat or dog.

- Write a joke book.

- Write a new nursery rhyme.

- Write a riddle book.

- Write a song.

Writing

Name: _____ Date: _____

Ways to Better Writing

Directions: Write a story about a big cat and a little dog. Try these ideas on a separate sheet of paper

❶ Make a list of things that could be funny. A cat could chase a dog. A cat could steal a dog's bone.

❷ Draw the story first. Make it like a comic strip.

❸ Write the story.

❹ Make the words fun. You could use new words for *big* and *little*. New words for *big* are *giant*, *great*, and *large*. New words for *little* are *small*, *mini*, *petite*, and *tiny*.

❺ Have a friend read the story. What else would make it more fun?

Name: _____ Date: _____

Ways to Better Listening

Directions: It takes practice to be a good listener. Play these games with a partner.

Player One: Hide a timer in the room.

Player Two: Find the timer when it goes off.

Player One: Sit in a chair with your eyes closed.

Player Two: Make the sound of an animal.

Player One: Tell what the animal is.

Player One: Make noise with two sticks.

Player Two: March until the noise stops.

Player One: Say an action like, "Stand up."

Player Two: Do the opposite.

Name: _____ Date: _____

Ways to Better Speaking and Listening

Directions: It takes practice to be a good speaker and listener. Play these games with a partner.

Player One: Look around the room. Choose something to describe. Say one clue like, "I see something blue."

Player Two: Ask something like, "Is it the ball?"

Player One: Add one more clue if the guess is wrong.

Player Two: Guess again. Keep going until the thing is guessed.

Player One: Say, "I got on the bus. I brought a _____."

Player Two: Repeat the first sentence and add something new.

Player One: Keep adding to the list. Start over when the list is too long.

Operations and Algebraic Thinking

Name: _____ Date: _____

Add Up the Apples!

Directions: Add up the apples to solve the problems.

❶

2 + 1 = 3

 + = 🍎🍎🍎

❷

2 + 2 = _____

🍎🍎 + 🍎🍎 = 🍎🍎🍎🍎

❸

3 + 2 = _____

🍎🍎🍎 + 🍎🍎 = 🍎🍎🍎🍎🍎

❹

1 + 2 = _____

🍎 + 🍎🍎 = 🍎🍎🍎

Operations and Algebraic Thinking

Name: _____ Date: _____

Add Up the Eggs!

Directions: Add up the eggs to solve the problems.

1

4 + 1 = 5

2

1 + 1 = _____

3

1 + 4 = _____

4

3 + 2 = _____

Name: _____ Date: _____

Count All of Those Bones!

Directions: Cross out bones to show the problem. Then, answer the questions.

1 The dog has 3 bones.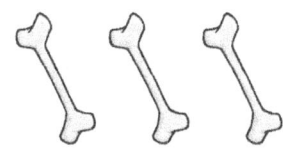

He ate 2 bones.

How many bones are left? _____

2 The dog has 4 bones.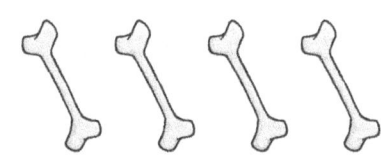

He ate 2 bones.

How many bones are left? _____

3 The dog has 5 bones.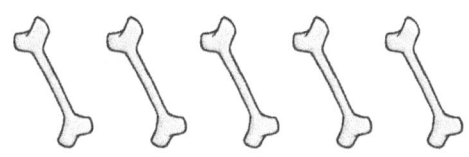

He ate 3 bones.

How many bones are left? _____

Name: _____ Date: _____

Count All of Those Nuts!

Directions: Cross out the nuts to show the problem. Then, answer the questions.

1 The squirrel has 6 nuts.

He ate 3 nuts.

How many nuts are left? _____

2 The squirrel has 7 nuts.

He ate 4 nuts.

How many nuts are left? _____

3 The squirrel has 7 nuts.

He ate 5 nuts.

How many nuts are left? _____

Name: _____ Date: _____

Count All of Those Stars!

Directions: Count the stars. Then, follow the steps.

❶

How many stars? _____

Draw 1 more. How many now? _____

❷

How many stars? _____

Draw 1 more. How many now? _____

❸

How many stars? _____

Draw 1 more. How many now? _____

Operations and Algebraic Thinking

Name: _____ Date: _____

Count All of Those Hats!

Directions: Count the hats. Then, follow the steps.

1

How many hats? _____

Draw 2 more. How many now? _____

2

How many hats? _____

Draw 3 more. How many now? _____

3

How many hats? _____

Draw 4 more. How many now? _____

Count All of Those Balls!

Directions: Count the balls. Then, follow the steps.

1

How many balls? _____

Draw 4 more. How many now? _____

2

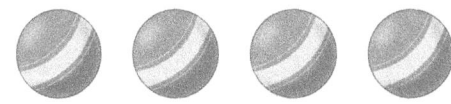

How many balls? _____

Draw 5 more. How many now? _____

3

How many balls? _____

Draw 2 more. How many now? _____

Name: _____ Date: _____

Counting Bones!

Directions: Count the bones. Then, follow the steps.

1

How many bones? _____

Draw 1 more. How many now? _____

2

How many bones? _____

Draw 8 more. How many now? _____

3

How many bones? _____

Draw 3 more. How many now? _____

Operations and Algebraic Thinking

Name: _____ Date: _____

Take Away Some Apples!

Directions: Count the apples. Then, follow the steps.

1

How many apples? _____

Cross out 1. How many are left? _____

2

How many apples? _____

Cross out 2. How many are left? _____

3

How many apples? _____

Cross out 3. How many are left? _____

Operations and Algebraic Thinking

Name: _____ Date: _____

Take Away Some Bats!

Directions: Count the bats. Then, follow the steps.

1

How many bats? _____

Cross out 3. How many are left? _____

2

How many bats? _____

Cross out 5. How many are left? _____

3

How many bats? _____

Cross out 4. How many are left? _____

Operations and Algebraic Thinking

Name: _____ Date: _____

Take Away Some Dogs!

Directions: Count the dogs. Then, follow the steps.

❶

How many dogs? _____

Cross out 2. How many are left? _____

❷

How many dogs? _____

Cross out 1. How many are left? _____

❸

How many dogs? _____

Cross out 5. How many are left? _____

Operations and Algebraic Thinking

Name: _____ Date: _____

Take Away Some Cats!

Directions: Count the cats. Then, follow the steps.

How many cats? _____

Cross out 3. How many are left? _____

How many cats? _____

Cross out 3. How many are left? _____

How many cats? _____

Cross out 0. How many are left? _____

Operations and Algebraic Thinking

Name: _____ Date: _____

Work with Numbers

Directions: Follow the steps below.

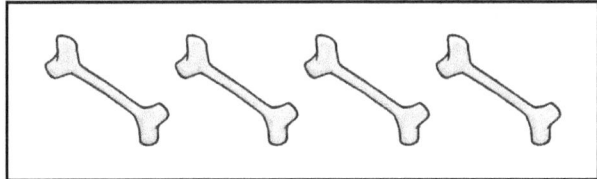 

_____ + _____ = _____
bones   bones   bones

❶ How many bones are in the first box? Write the number on the first line.

❷ Draw 1 bone in the other box. Write the number on the second line.

❸ How many bones are there in all? Write the number on the last line.

69

Operations and Algebraic Thinking

Name: _____ Date: _____

Work with More Numbers

Directions: Draw more hats. Then, solve each problem.

1.

Draw 2 hats.

_____ + _____ = _____
 hats   hats   hats

2.

Draw 3 hats.

_____ + _____ = _____
 hats   hats   hats

Operations and Algebraic Thinking

Name: _____ Date: _____

Add Some Logs

Directions: Draw more logs. Then, solve each problem.

1

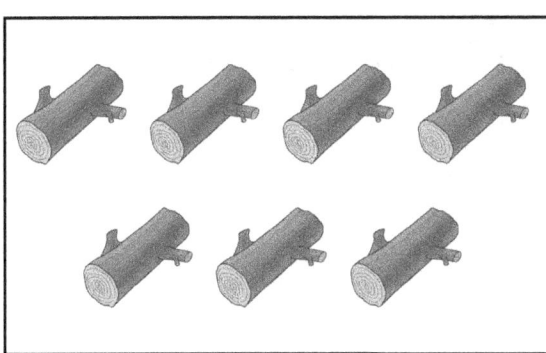

_____ + _____ = _____
 logs   log   logs

2

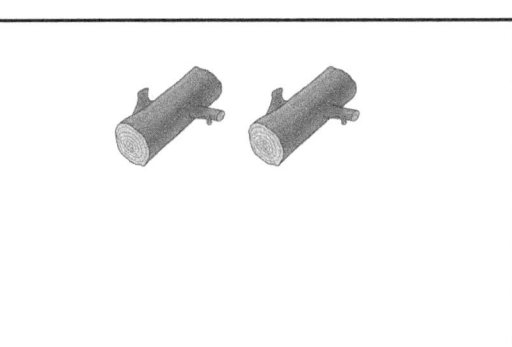 Draw 2 logs.

_____ + _____ = _____
 logs   logs   logs

71

Operations and Algebraic Thinking

Name: _____ Date: _____

Find 10 Eggs

Directions: Draw more eggs. Then, solve each problem.

 1.

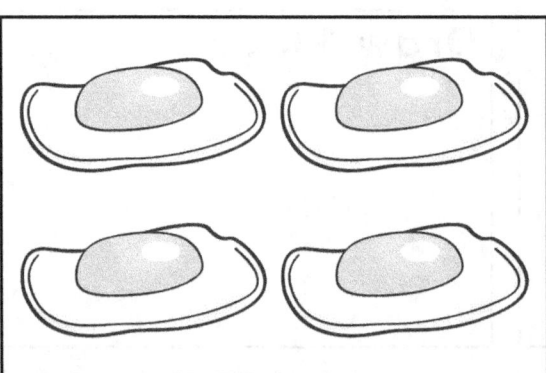

Draw 2 eggs.

_____ + _____ = _____
 eggs   eggs   eggs

2.

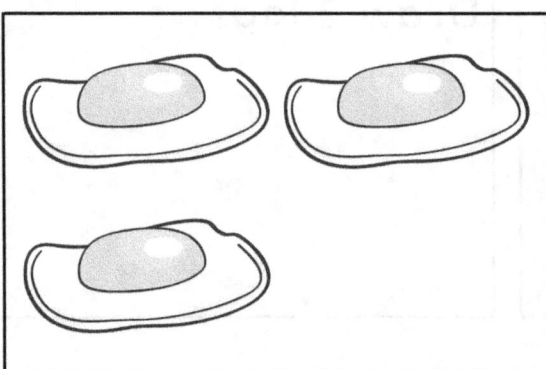

Draw 3 eggs.

_____ + _____ = _____
 eggs   eggs   eggs

Operations and Algebraic Thinking

Name: _____ Date: _____

What's the Problem?

Directions: Write the answer to each problem.

1. ☀ ☀ + ☀ = __3__ suns

2. ☀ ☀ ☀ + ☀ ☀ = ____ suns

3. ☀ + ☀ ☀ ☀ ☀ = ____ suns

4. ☀ ☀ + ☀ ☀ = ____ suns

5. ☀ + ☀ ☀ ☀ = ____ suns

Operations and Algebraic Thinking

Name: _____ Date: _____

Finish the Problems

Directions: Follow the steps to solve each problem.

1

_____ - _____ = _____

Cross out 1 star. How many stars are left?

2

_____ - _____ = _____

Cross out 2 stars. How many stars are left?

3

_____ - _____ = _____

Cross out 3 stars. How many stars are left?

Number and Operations in Base Ten

Name: _____ Date: _____

Big Problems with Bugs!

Directions: Count the bugs in the first box and second box. Write the numbers. Then, add the bugs.

1

_____ + _____ = _____

2
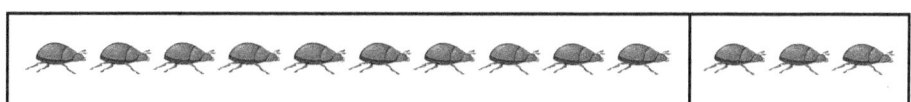

_____ + _____ = _____

3

_____ + _____ = _____

4

_____ + _____ = _____

Number and Operations in Base Ten

Name: _____ Date: _____

Big Problems with Ants!

Directions: Count the ants in the first box and second box. Write the numbers. Then, add the ants.

1

_____ + _____ = _____

2

_____ + _____ = _____

3

_____ + _____ = _____

4

_____ + _____ = _____

Measurement and Data

Name: _____ Date: _____

Measure Up!

Directions: Measure the items below with pencils.

Items to measure	Length with pencils
❶	_____ pencils
❷	_____ pencils
❸	_____ pencil

77

Measurement and Data

Name: _____ Date: _____

Measure and Compare

Directions: Find the items below. Measure the items with your finger. Have a friend do the same thing.

Items to measure	Length with my fingers	Length with my friend's fingers
	_____ fingers	_____ fingers
	_____ fingers	_____ fingers
	_____ fingers	_____ fingers

Name: _____ Date: _____

Measure and Compare More

Directions: Measure the items below with paper clips.

Items to measure	Length with paper clips
2 + 2 = 4 + 3 = 7 + 3 = a b c d e f g	_____ paper clips
(flag)	_____ paper clips
(block A B C)	_____ paper clips

Measurement and Data

Name: _____ Date: _____

Measure and Compare Big Things

Directions: Find these items. Measure the items with your hand. Have a friend do the same thing.

Items to measure	Length with my hands	Length with my friend's hands
(baseball bat)	_____ hands	_____ hands
(bicycle)	_____ hands	_____ hands
(flag)	_____ hands	_____ hands

Measurement and Data

Name: _____ Date: _____

Sort and Count!

Directions: Answer the questions.

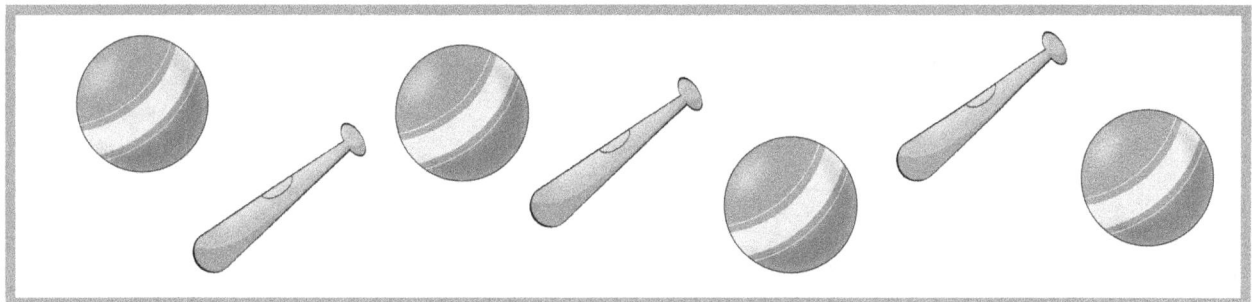

❶ Count the balls. How many? _____

❷ Count the bats. How many? _____

❸ Count the suns. How many? _____

❹ Count the clouds. How many? _____

81

Measurement and Data

Name: _____ Date: _____

Sort and Count More!

Directions: Answer the questions.

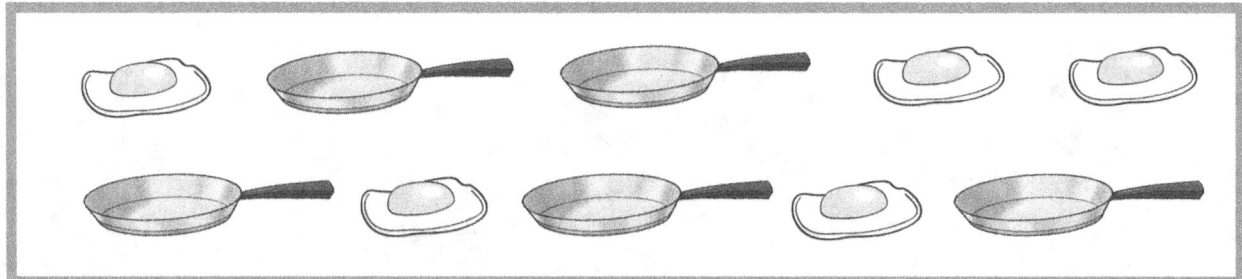

❶ Count the pans. How many? _____

❷ Count the eggs. How many? _____

❸ Count the stars. How many? _____

❹ Count the moons. How many? _____

Measurement and Data

Name: _____ Date: _____

Sort and Count by Size

Directions: Answer the questions.

❶ Count the little cars. How many? _____

❷ Count the big cars. How many? _____

❸ Count the big dogs. How many? _____

❹ Count the little dogs. How many? _____

83

Measurement and Data

Name: _____ Date: _____

Sort and Count by Shape

Directions: Answer the questions.

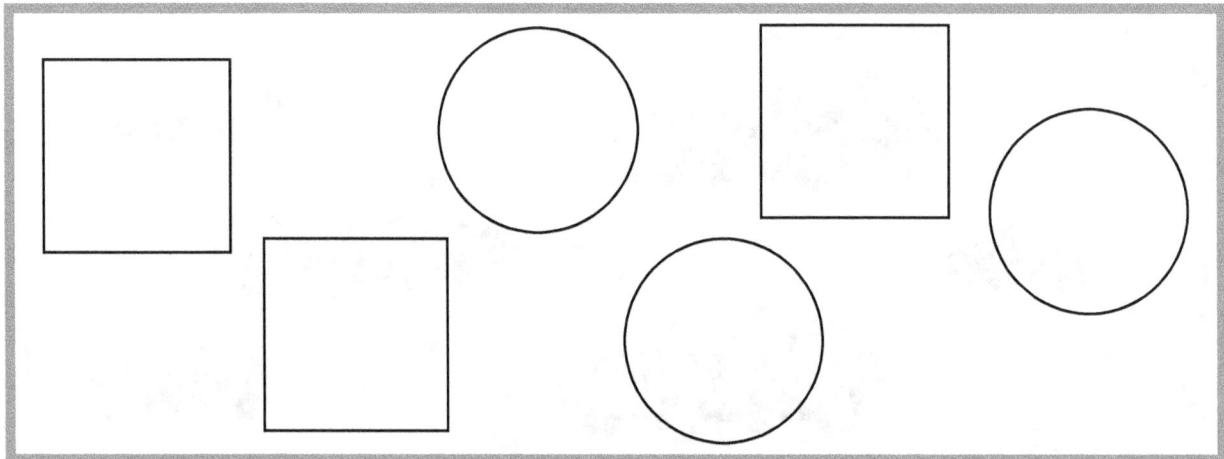

❶ Count the circles. How many? _____

❷ Count the squares. How many? _____

❸ Count the food things. How many? _____

❹ Count the play things. How many? _____

Geometry

Name: _____ Date: _____

Find the Shapes

Directions: Look at the picture. Then, answer the questions.

❶ What shape is the sign?

    a. square

    b. rectangle

    c. circle

❷ Where is the man?

    a. above the car

    b. next to the car

    c. under the car

❸ What shape is the cash?

    a. square

    b. rectangle

    c. circle

❹ Where is the cloud?

    a. in front of the car

    b. above the car

    c. under the car

Geometry

Name: _____ Date: _____

Find More Shapes

Directions: Look at the picture. Then, answer the questions.

❶ What shape is the art?

a. square
b. rectangle
c. circle

❷ What shape is the rug?

a. circle
b. rectangle
c. square

❸ Where is the rug?

a. above the bed
b. behind the bed
c. under the bed

❹ Where is the art?

a. on the floor
b. on the wall
c. on the bed

Geometry

Name: _____ Date: _____

Where Are the Shapes?

Directions: Look at the picture. Then, answer the questions.

❶ What shape are the windows?

   a. square

   b. rectangle

   c. circle

❷ What shape is the door?

   a. circle

   b. rectangle

   c. square

❸ Where is the grass?

   a. above the house

   b. in front of the house

   c. on the door

❹ Where is the door?

   a. on the top of the house

   b. under the house

   c. by a window

Geometry

Name: _____ Date: _____

Name the Shapes

Directions: Draw a line from each shape to its name.

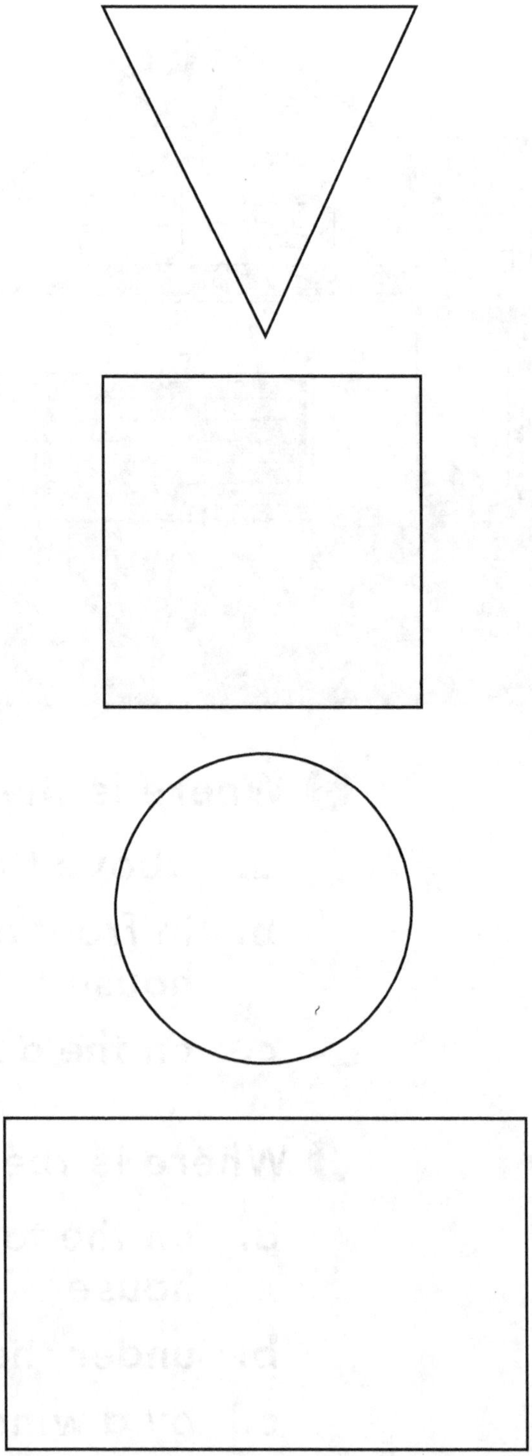

square

rectangle

circle

triangle

Name: _____ Date: _____

Shape Match

Directions: Draw a line from each shape to its name.

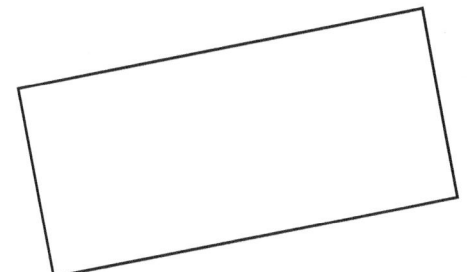   square

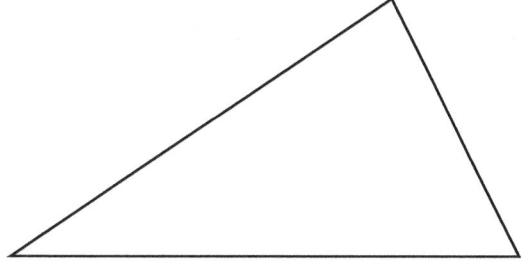   rectangle

   circle

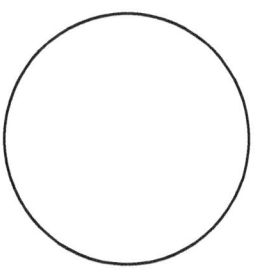   triangle

Geometry

Name: _____ Date: _____

More Shape Naming

Directions: Color the squares red. Color the triangles green. Color the circles blue. Color the rectangles yellow.

Geometry

Name: _____ Date: _____

Build with Shapes

Directions: Follow the steps.

❶ Outline the star in yellow.

❷ Outline the triangles in green.

❸ Outline the rectangles in black.

❹ Outline the squares in blue.

❺ Outline the circle in red.

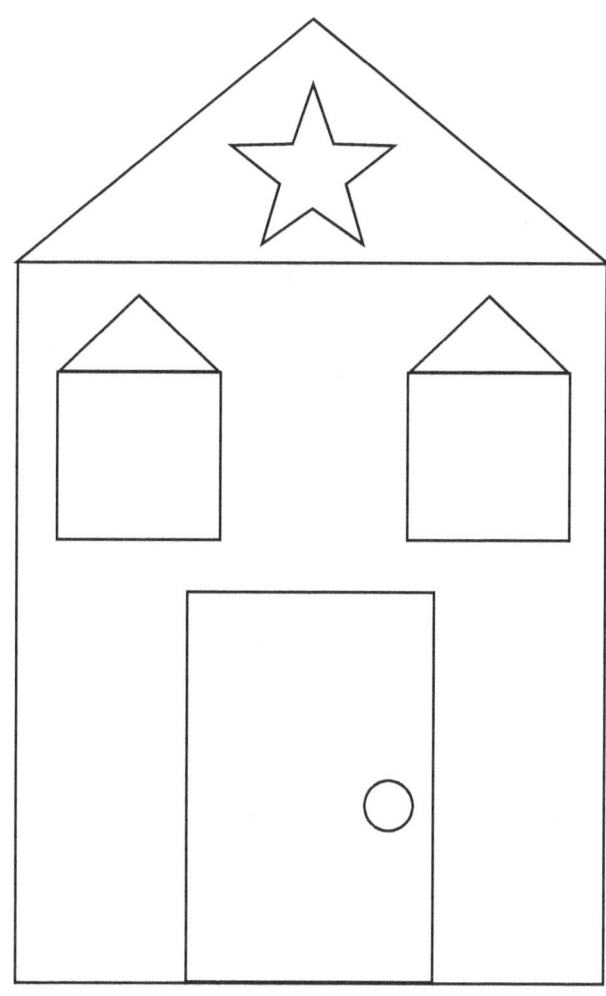

91

Answer Key

How Many Parts? (page 4)
1. 1
2. 2
3. 1
4. 1
5. 1
6. 2

What Is That Sound? (page 5)
1. ball, bed
2. cat, can
3. dog
4. fan, fox

Name That Letter Sound (page 6)
1. kite, key
2. leaf, leg
3. mop, milk
4. nose, nest, net

Name More Letter Sounds (page 7)
1. sun, scissors
2. turtle
3. vest
4. whale, wig

Practice Your Letters (page 8)
Students should have traced the letters correctly.

Practice More Letters (page 9)
Students should have traced the letters correctly.

Practice Even More Letters (page 10)
Students should have traced the letters correctly.

Lots of Letters (page 11)
Students should have traced the letters correctly.

Trace More Letters (page 12)
Students should have traced the letters correctly.

Keep Tracing (page 13)
Students should have traced the letters correctly.

Which Word Is Right? (page 14)
1. bat
2. can
3. Dad
4. Mom

Choose the Right Word (page 15)
1. dog
2. baby
3. bird
4. bus

Which Word? (page 16)
1. hen
2. pen
3. house
4. book

Choose More Words (page 17)
1. ant
2. dish
3. nest
4. tub

Answer Key *(cont.)*

Finish the Sentence (page 18)
1. flaps
2. wags
3. swims
4. hops

What Do These Pictures Say? (page 19)
1. rides
2. runs
3. naps
4. reads

Read Carefully! (page 20)
1. moves
2. skips
3. stops
4. flies

Read These Carefully! (page 21)
1. plays
2. hugs
3. draws
4. rests

One or Two? (page 22)
1. pig
2. hats
3. pans
4. sun

More Than One? (page 23)
1. bed
2. apples
3. can
4. nuts

How Many in These? (page 24)
1. foxes
2. watches
3. bone
4. brush

More Plural Practice (page 25)
1. tree
2. sock
3. locks
4. coat

Finish the Questions (page 26)
1. What
2. Who
3. What
4. Who

Finish More Questions (page 27)
1. Where
2. Who
3. Who
4. Where

Where Is It? (page 28)
1. on
2. by
3. on
4. by

Where Are They? (page 29)
1. in
2. by
3. by
4. in

Answer Key (cont.)

Capital Mistake (page 30)
1. i have a dog.
2. my dog has spots.
3. May i pet your dog?
4. your dog is big!

Capitalize It (page 31)
I, They, I, Max, He, She

Punctuate the Sentences (page 32)
1. ?
2. !
3. .
4. ?

Punctuate More Sentences (page 33)
Suggested punctuation: Do you know how to snap? I do. It can be hard. I like to snap!

Name the Short Vowels (page 34)
1. a
2. o
3. a
4. e

Name More Short Vowels (page 35)
1. a
2. i
3. u
4. o

Spelling Fun (page 36)
1. car
2. sun
3. leg
4. cap

More Spelling Words (page 37)
1. egg
2. pig
3. can
4. dad or man

Keep Spelling! (page 38)
1. cap
2. pan
3. wig
4. ham

Keep Spelling More Words! (page 39)
1. foot
2. ball
4. ring
5. duck

Find the Answers (page 40)
1. c
2. c
3. a
4. a

Questions to Answer (page 41)
1. b
2. c
3. b
4. b

Read the Answer (page 42)
1. b
2. c
3. b
4. a

Answer Key *(cont.)*

Book Log (page 43)
Students' responses will vary.

Opposite Characters (page 44)
Students' responses will vary.

Be a Great Reader! (page 45)
Students' responses will vary.

More Tips for Being a Great Reader (page 46)
Students' responses will vary.

My Good Book! (page 47)
Students' responses will vary.

My Book Review (page 48)
Students' responses will vary.

About a Pet (page 49)
Students' responses will vary.

My Review (page 50)
Students' responses will vary.

My Best Day (page 51)
Students' responses will vary.

My Funny Day (page 52)
Students' responses will vary.

Writing Ideas (page 53)
Students' responses will vary.

Ways to Better Writing (page 54)
Students' responses will vary.

Ways to Better Listening (page 55)
Students' responses will vary.

Ways to Better Speaking and Listening (page 56)
Students' responses will vary.

Add Up the Apples! (page 57)
1. 3 apples
2. 4 apples
3. 5 apples
4. 3 apples

Add Up the Eggs! (page 58)
1. 5 eggs
2. 2 eggs
3. 5 eggs
4. 5 eggs

Count All of Those Bones! (page 59)
1. 1 bone
2. 2 bones
3. 2 bones

Count All of Those Nuts! (page 60)
1. 3 nuts
2. 3 nuts
3. 2 nuts

Count All of Those Stars! (page 61)
1. 3; 4
2. 5; 6
3. 4; 5

Count All of Those Hats! (page 62)
1. 6; 8
2. 6; 9
3. 4; 8

Answer Key (cont.)

Count All of Those Balls! (page 63)
1. 3; 7
2. 4; 9
3. 7; 9

Counting Bones! (page 64)
1. 9; 10
2. 1; 9
3. 7; 10

Take Away Some Apples! (page 65)
1. 6; 5
2. 8; 6
3. 4; 1

Take Away Some Bats! (page 66)
1. 7; 4
2. 9; 4
3. 8; 4

Take Away Some Dogs! (page 67)
1. 8; 6
2. 9; 8
3. 8; 3

Take Away Some Cats! (page 68)
1. 10; 7
2. 9; 6
3. 7; 7

Work with Numbers (page 69)
4 + 1 = 5

Work with More Numbers (page 70)
6 + 2 = 8
5 + 3 = 8

Add Some Logs (page 71)
7 + 1 = 8
2 + 2 = 4

Add Some Eggs (page 72)
4 + 2 = 6
3 + 3 = 6

What's the Problem? (page 73)
1. 3
2. 5
3. 5
4. 4
5. 4

Finish the Problems (page 74)
1. 3 − 1 = 2
2. 5 − 2 = 3
3. 3 − 3 = 0

Big Problems with Bugs! (page 75)
1. 10 + 1 = 11
2. 10 + 3 = 13
3. 10 + 5 = 15
4. 10 + 7 = 17

Big Problems with Ants! (page 76)
1. 10 + 2 = 12
2. 10 + 4 = 14
3. 10 + 9 = 19
4. 10 + 6 = 16

Measure Up! (page 77)
1. 2 pencils
2. 6 pencils
3. 1 pencil

Answer Key (cont.)

Measure and Compare (page 78)

Students' responses will vary.

Measure and Compare More (page 79)

1. 10 paper clips
2. 4 paper clips
3. 3 paper clips

Measure and Compare Big Things (page 80)

Students' responses will vary.

Sort and Count! (page 81)

1. 4 balls
2. 3 bats
3. 6 suns
4. 4 clouds

Sort and Count More! (page 82)

1. 5 pans
2. 5 eggs
3. 5 stars
4. 4 moons

Sort and Count by Size (page 83)

1. 3 little cars
2. 3 big cars
3. 5 big dogs
4. 3 little dogs

Sort and Count by Shape (page 84)

1. 3 circles
2. 3 squares
3. 3 food things
4. 4 play things

Find the Shapes (page 85)

1. b
2. b
3. b
4. b

Find More Shapes (page 86)

1. a
2. a
3. c
4. b

Where Are the Shapes? (page 87)

1. a
2. b
3. b
4. c

Name the Shapes (page 88)

Students should connect the names to the appropriate shapes.

Shape Match (page 89)

Students should connect the names to the appropriate shapes.

More Shape Naming (page 90)

Check activity sheets to see that students followed instructions.

Build with Shapes (page 91)

Check activity sheets to see that students followed instructions.

A Topix Media Lab Publication
For inquiries, call 646-476-8860

CEO Tony Romando

Senior Vice President of Sales & New Markets Tom Mifsud
Vice President of Retail Sales & Logistics Linda Greenblatt
Director of Finance Vandana Patel
Manufacturing Director Nancy Puskuldjian
Financial Analyst Matthew Quinn
Brand Marketing & Promotions Assistant Emily McBride

Chief Content Officer Jeff Ashworth
Director of Editorial Operations Courtney Kerrigan
Creative Director Steven Charny
Photo Director Dave Weiss
Executive Editor Tim Baker

Art Director Susan Dazzo
Senior Editor Trevor Courneen
Designer Kelsey Payne
Associate Editor Juliana Sharaf
Copy Editor & Fact Checker Tara Sherman

Co-Founders Bob Lee, Tony Romando

Published by arrangement with Teacher Created Materials, Inc.

Topix Media Lab Special #1, 2020. TCM Bright and Brainy Kindergarten Learning published by Topix Media Lab, 14 Wall Street, Suite 4B, New York, NY 10005. All rights reserved. No material in this issue may be reprinted without the written permission of the publisher. Entire contents copyright © 2020. Certain photographs used in this publication are used by license or permission from the owner thereof, or are otherwise publicly available. This publication is not endorsed by any person or entity appearing herein. Any product names, logos, brands or other trademarks featured or referred to in the publication are the property of their respective trademark owners. Topix Media Lab is not affiliated with, nor sponsored or endorsed by, any of the persons, entities, product names, logos, brands or other trademarks featured or referred to in any of its publications. PRINTED IN THE USA.

Cover illustrations: Shutterstock

QW D20 1

ISBN: 9781948174695

www.ingramcontent.com/pod-product-compliance
Lightning Source LLC
Chambersburg PA
CBHW051807100526
44592CB00016B/2602